CW00422142

My Ultimate Pescatarian Diet Plan

Seafood and Vegetarian Delicious Dishes
for Healthy Everyday Meals

Lara Dillard

© copyright 2021 – all rights reserved.

he content contained within this book may not be eproduced, duplicated or transmitted without direct vritten permission from the author or the publisher.

under no circumstances will any blame or legal esponsibility be held against the publisher, or author, or any damages, reparation, or monetary loss due to he information contained within this book. either lirectly or indirectly.

egal notice:

his book is copyright protected. this book is only for personal use. you cannot amend, distribute, sell, use, quote or paraphrase any part, or the content within this book, without the consent of the author or publisher.

disclaimer notice:

please note the information contained within this document is for educational and entertainment purposes only. all effort has been executed to present accurate, up to date, and reliable, complete information. no warranties of any kind are declared or mplied. readers acknowledge that the author is not engaging in the rendering of legal, financial, medical or professional advice. the content within this book has been derived from various sources. please consult a censed professional before attempting

any techniques outlined in this book.

by reading this document, the reader agrees that under no circumstances is the author responsible for any losses, direct or indirect, which are incurred as a result of the use of information contained within this document, including, but not limited to, — errors, omissions, or inaccuracies.

Table of Contents

Shrimp Creole

Servings: 6

Total Time: 4 Hours 15 Minutes

Calories: 346

Fat: 3.2 g

Protein: 39 g

Carbs: 38.9 g

Ingredients and Quantity

- 1 1/4 cups onion, chopped
- 1 garlic clove, crushed and minced
- 1 cup red bell pepper, chopped
- 1 1/2 cups celery, diced
- 1 tsp. salt
- 1/4 tsp. pepper
- 6 drops Tabasco
- 1/2 tsp. Creole seasoning

- 8 oz. canned tomato sauce
- 28 oz. canned whole tomatoes, crushed
- 2 lb. shrimp, deveined and shell removed
- 1 cup white rice, cooked

Direction

1. Add all the ingredients to the slow cooker, except for the shrimp.
2. Cook on High for 4 hours.
3. In the last 30 minutes of your cooking, add the shrimp.
4. Put hot, cooked rice in a bowl.
5. Top with the shrimp. Serve and enjoy!

Salmon and Scalloped Potatoes

Servings: 9

Total Time: 9 Hours 15 Minutes

Calories: 174

Fat: 4.2 g

Protein: 12.4 g

Carbs: 22.2 g

Ingredients and Quantity

- Cooking spray
- 3 tbsp. flour
- Salt and pepper, to taste
- 16 oz. salmon, drained and shredded into flakes
- 5 potatoes, sliced
- 1/2 cup onion, chopped
- 1/4 cup water
- 10 oz. cream of mushroom soup

- Pinch of nutmeg

Direction

1. Grease your slow cooker with cooking spray.
2. Sprinkle with a little bit of flour.
3. Sprinkle with salt and pepper.
4. Arrange a layer of half of the salmon flakes, half of the potatoes, and half of the chopped onions.
5. Make another set of layers.
6. In a bowl, mix the water and soup.
7. Pour into the slow cooker. Add the nutmeg.
8. Cover the pot. Cook on low for 9 hours. Serve and enjoy!

Tilapia in Lemon Pepper Sauce

Servings: 4

Total Time: 2 Hours 30 Minutes

Calories: 172

Fat: 7.2 g

Protein: 23.6 g

Carbs: 4.7 g

Ingredients and Quantity

- 4 fillets tilapia
- 16 spears asparagus
- 8 tbsp. freshly squeezed lemon juice
- 8 tbsp. pepper
- 2 tbsp. almond butter

Direction

1. Cut a foil that's large enough to wrap around the tilapia fillet.
2. Put each tilapia fillet into a foil.
3. Place 4 spears of asparagus on each tilapia.
4. Sprinkle each fillet with ¼ teaspoon pepper.
5. Sprinkle 2 tablespoons lemon juice onto each fillet.
6. Add ½ tablespoon butter on each fillet.
7. Wrap the fillet with the foil.
8. Place wrapped tilapia in the slow cooker.
9. Put on the lid and cook on High for 2 hours. Serve and enjoy!

Shrimp Scampi

Servings: 4

Total Time: 2 Hours 10 Minutes

Calories: 180

Fat: 7.1 g

Protein: 21.5 g

Carbs: 3.5 g

Ingredients and Quantity

- 1/2 cup white wine
- 1/4 cup reduced sodium chicken stock
- 2 tbsp. freshly squeezed lemon juice
- 2 tsp. parsley, minced
- 2 tsp. garlic, chopped2 tbsp. olive oil
- 1 lb. large shrimp (about 16 to 20 pieces)

Direction

1. Mix all the ingredients in a large bowl.
2. Transfer to the slow cooker.
3. Cook on low for 2 hours.
4. Serve in bowls. Enjoy!

Air Fried Zucchini Chips

Servings: 3

Total Time: 20 Minutes

Calories: 187

Fat: 6.6 g

Protein: 10.8 g

Carbs: 21.1 g

Ingredients and Quantity

- 1 cup panko bread crumbs
- 3/4 grated vegan cheese
- 1 medium zucchini, sliced thinly
- 3 tbsp. apple sauce

Direction

1. Place the Ninja Foodi Cook and Crisp basket in the ceramic pot.
2. Mix the panko bread crumbs and parmesan cheese. Set aside.
3. Dip the zucchini in apple sauce before dredging in the panko mixture.
4. Place the dredged zucchini in the basket.
5. Close the crisping lid and press the Air Crisp button before pressing the START button.
6. Adjust the cooking time to 15 minutes. Serve and enjoy!

Crispy Cauliflower Bites

Servings: 4

Total Time: 12 Minutes

Calories: 130

Fat: 7 g

Protein: 4.3 g

Carbs: 12.4 g

Ingredients and Quantity

- 3 garlic cloves, minced
- 1 tbsp. olive oil
- 1/2 tsp. salt
- 1/2 tsp. smoked paprika
- 4 cups cauliflower florets

Direction

1. Place in the ceramic pot the Foodi Cook and Crisp basket.
2. Place all ingredients in a bowl and toss to combine.
3. Place the seasoned cauliflower florets in the basket.
4. Close the crisping lid and press the Air Crisp button before pressing the START button.
5. Adjust the cooking time to 10 minutes.
6. Give the basket a shake while cooking for even cooking. Serve and enjoy!

Baked Bananas

Servings: 4

Total Time: 12 Minutes

Calories: 183

Fat: 0.9 g

Protein: 1.4 g

Carbs: 42.2 g

Ingredients and Quantity

- 4 firm bananas, peeled and halved
- 1/4 cup maple syrup
- 1 tbsp. ground cinnamon
- 1 piece fresh ginger, grated
- 1 1/2 tsp. nutmeg

Direction

1. Place in the ceramic pot the Foodi Cook and Crisp reversible rack.
2. In a bowl, season the bananas with maple syrup, ground cinnamon, ginger, and nutmeg.
3. Place the bananas on the rack.
4. Close the crisping lid and press the Bake/Roast button before pressing the START button.
5. Adjust the cooking time to 10 minutes. Serve and enjoy!

Spicy Roasted Broccoli

Servings: 2

Total Time: 23 Minutes

Calories: 76

Fat: 3.9 g

Protein: 2.1 g

Carbs: 8 g

Ingredients and Quantity

- 2 cups broccoli florets
- 1 yellow bell pepper, sliced
- 1 tsp. garlic powder
- 1 tbsp. steak seasoning
- 2 tsp. chili powder
- 1 tbsp. extra virgin olive oil
- Salt and pepper, to taste

Direction

1. Place in the ceramic pot the Foodi Cook and Crisp basket insert.
2. Toss all ingredients in a mixing bowl.
3.
4. Place the vegetables in the basket.
5. Close the crisping lid and press the Bake/Roast button before pressing the START button.
6. Adjust the cooking time to 20 minutes.
7. Give the basket a shake to roast the veggies evenly. Serve and enjoy!

Quinoa and Potato Salad

Servings: 6

Total Time: 25 Minutes

Ingredients and Quantity

- 1/4 cup white balsamic vinegar
- 1 tbsp. Dijon mustard
- 1 tsp. sweet paprika
- 1/2 tsp. ground black pepper
- 1/4 tsp. celery seeds
- 1/4 tsp. salt
- 1/4 cup olive oil
- 1 1/2 pounds tiny white potatoes, halved
- 1 cup blond (white) quinoa
- 1 medium shallot, minced
- 2 medium celery stalks, thinly sliced
- 1 large dill pickle, diced

Direction

1. Whisk the vinegar, mustard, paprika, pepper, celery seeds and salt in a large serving bowl until smooth.

2. Whisk in the olive oil in a thin, steady stream until the dressing is fairly creamy.

3. Place the potatoes and quinoa in the Ninja Foodi Multicooker; add enough cold tap water so that the ingredients are submerged by 3 inches (some of the quinoa may float).

4. Lock the lid on the Ninja Foodi Multicooker and then cook for 10 minutes. To get 10-minutes cook time, press "Pressure" button and use the Time Adjustment button to adjust the cook time to 10 minutes.

5. Use the quick-release method to bring the pot's pressure back to normal.

6. Unlock and open the pot. Close the crisping lid.

7. Select BROIL, and set the time to 5 minutes. Select START/STOP to begin.

8. Cook until top has browned.

9. Drain the contents of the pot into a colander lined with paper towels or into a fine-mesh sieve in the sink. Do not rinse.

10.   Transfer the potatoes and quinoa to the large bowl with the dressing.

11.   Add the shallot, celery, and pickle; toss gently and set aside for a minute or two to warm up the vegetables. Serve and enjoy!

Buttery Carrots with Pancetta

Servings: 5

Total Time: 20 Minutes

Ingredients and Quantity

- 4 oz. pancetta, diced
- 1 medium leek, white and pale green parts only, sliced lengthwise, washed and thinly sliced
- 1/4 cup moderately sweet white wine (I used dry Riesling)
- 1 pound baby carrots
- 1/2 tsp. ground black pepper
- 2 tbsp. almond butter, cut into small bits

Direction

1. Put the pancetta in the Ninja Foodi turned to the Air Crisp function.
2. Use time adjustment button to set cooking time to 5 minutes.
3. Add the leeks; cook, often stirring, until softened.

4. Pour in the wine and scrape up any browned bits at the bottom of the pot as it comes to a simmer.

5. Add the carrots and pepper; stir well.

6. Scrape and pour the contents of the Ninja Food Multicooker into a 1-quart, round, high-sided soufflé or baking dish. Dot with the bits of butter.

7. Lay a piece of parchment paper on top of the dish, then a piece of aluminum foil.

8. Seal the foil tightly over the baking dish.

9. Set the Ninja Foodi Multicooker rack inside, and pour in 2 cups water.

10. Use aluminum foil to build a sling for the baking dish; lower the baking dish into the cooker.

11. Lock the lid on the Ninja Foodi Multicooker and then cook for 7 minutes. To get 7-minutes cook time, press "Pressure" button and use the Time Adjustment button to adjust the cook time to 7 minutes.

12. Use the quick-release method to return the pot's pressure to normal.

13. Close the crisping lid. Select BROIL, and set the time to 5 minutes.

14.   Select START/STOP to begin. Cook until top has browned.

15.   Unlock and open the pot. Use the foil sling to lift the baking dish out of the cooker.

16.   Uncover and stir well. Serve and enjoy!

Almond Butter Spaghetti Squash

Servings: 6

Total Time: 25 Minutes

Ingredients and Quantity

- One 3 1/2 pound spaghetti squash
- 6 tbsp. almond butter
- 2 tbsp. packed fresh sage leaves, minced
- 1/2 tsp. salt
- 1/2 tsp. ground black pepper
- 1/2 cup finely grated vegan cheese (about 1 oz.)

Direction

1. Put the squash with the cut side facing up in the cooker. Then add 1 cup water.

2. Lock the lid on the Ninja Foodi and then cook for 12 minutes.
3. Use the quick-release method to bring the pot's pressure back to normal.
4. Unlock and open the cooker. Transfer the squash halves to a cutting board; cool for 10 minutes.
5. Discard the liquid in the cooker.
6. Use a fork to scrape the spaghetti-like flesh off the skin and onto the cutting board; discard the skins.
7. Melt the butter in the electric cooker turned to its browning function.
8. Stir in the sage, salt, and pepper, then add all of the squash.
9. Stir and toss over the heat until well combined and heated through about 2 minutes.
10.   Add the cheese, toss well. Close the crisping lid.
11.   Select BROIL, and set the time to 5 minutes.
12.   Select START/STOP to begin.
13.   Cook until top has browned. Serve and enjoy!

Rye Berry and Celery Root Salad

Servings: 6

Total Time: 45 Minutes

Ingredients and Quantity

- 3/4 cup rye berries
- 1 medium celeriac (celery root), peeled and shredded through the large holes of a box grater
- 2 tbsp. almond butter
- 2 tbsp. maple syrup
- 2 tbsp. apple cider vinegar
- 1/2 tsp. salt
- 1/2 tsp. ground black pepper

Direction

1. Place the rye berries in the Foodi; pour in enough cold tap water, so the grains are submerged by 2 inches.
2. Lock the lid on the Foodi and then cook for 40 minutes.
3. Pressure Release. Use the quick-release method to bring the pot's pressure back to normal.
4. Unlock and open the cooker. Stir in the shredded celeriac.
5. Cover the pot without locking it and set aside for 1 minute.
6. Drain the pot into a large colander set in the sink.
7. Wipe out the cooker. Melt the butter in the Foodi; turned to it sauté function.
8. Add the maple syrup and cook for 1 minute, constantly stirring.
9. Add the drained rye berries and celeriac; cook, constantly stirring, for 1 minute.
10.   10.Stir in the vinegar, salt, and pepper to serve. Enjoy!

Crispy Tofu

Servings: 4

Total Time: 60 Minutes

Calories: 137

Fat: 3.4 g

Protein: 2.3 g

Carbs: 24 g

Ingredients and Quantity

- 1 tsp. seasoned rice vinegar
- 2 tbsp. low sodium soy sauce
- 2 tsp. toasted sesame oil
- 1 block firm tofu, sliced into cubes
- 1 tbsp. potato starch
- Cooking spray

Direction

1. In a bowl, mix the vinegar, soy sauce, and sesame oil.
2. Marinate the tofu for 30 minutes.
3. Coat the tofu with potato starch.
4. Spray the Ninja Foodi basket with oil.
5. Seal the crisping lid.
6. Choose the air crisp setting.
7. Cook at 370 degrees for 20 minutes, flipping halfway through.
8. You can serve with soy sauce and vinegar dipping sauce. Enjoy!

Onion Rings

Servings: 4

Total Time: 40 Minutes

Calories: 147

Fat: 11.3 g

Protein: 2.6 g

Carbs: 10.9 g

Ingredients and Quantity

- 3 yellow onions, sliced into rings
- 1/2 cup almond flour
- 2/3 cup unsweetened coconut milk
- 1/2 tsp. paprika
- 1/4 tsp. turmeric
- Salt, to taste

Direction

1. Mix all the ingredients except the onion rings in a large bowl.
2. Coat each onion ring with the mixture.
3. Place in the Ninja Foodi basket.
4. Seal the crisping lid.
5. Set it to air crisp.
6. Cook at 400 degrees for 10 minutes, flipping halfway through.
7. You can serve with ketchup or hot sauce. Enjoy!

Potato Wedges

Servings: 4

Total Time: 40 Minutes

Calories: 179

Fat: 2.6 g

Protein: 2.8 g

Carbs: 36.2 g

Ingredients and Quantity

- 1 lb. potatoes, sliced into wedges
- 1 tsp. olive oil
- Salt and pepper, to taste
- 1/2 tsp. garlic powder

Direction

1. Coat the potatoes with oil.
2. Season with salt, pepper and garlic powder

3. Add the potatoes in the Ninja Foodi basket.

4. Cover with the crisping lid.

5. Set it to air crisp.

6. Cook at 400 degrees F for 16 minutes, flipping halfway through.

7. You can serve with vegan cheese sauce. Enjoy!

Garlic Chips

Servings: 2

Total Time: 70 Minutes

Calories: 156

Fat: 0.2 g

Protein: 4 g

Carbs: 35.4 g

Ingredients and Quantity

- **P**otatoes, sliced into chips
- Salt, to taste
- 4 garlic cloves
- 4 garlic cloves, minced
- 2 tbsp. vegan cheese

Direction

1. Put the potatoes in a bowl of water
2. Stir in the salt.
3. Soak for 20 to 30 minutes.
4. Drain the potatoes and pat try.
5. Season with the garlic and vegan cheese.
6. Arrange the chips on the Ninja Foodi basket.
7. Seal the crisping lid.
8. Set it to air crisp function.
9. Cook at 350 degrees for 10 minutes or until crispy.
10. Flip every 3 to 5 minutes.
11. You can serve with hot sauce or mayo. Enjoy!

Cauliflower Stir Fry

Servings: 4

Total Time: 40 Minutes

Calories: 93

Fat: 3 g

Protein: 4 g

Carbs: 12 g

Ingredients and Quantity

- 1 head cauliflower, sliced into florets
- 3/4 cup white onion, sliced
- 5 garlic cloves, minced
- 1 1/2 tsp. tamari
- 1 tbsp. rice vinegar
- 1/2 tsp. coconut sugar
- 1 tbsp. coconut cream

Direction

1. Put the cauliflower in the Ninja Foodi basket.
2. Seal the crisping lid.
3. Select the air crisp setting.
4. Cook at 350 degrees F for 10 minutes.
5. Add the onion, stir and cook for additional 10 minutes.
6. Add the garlic, and cook for 5 minutes.
7. Mix the rest of the ingredients.
8. Pour over the cauliflower before serving.
9. You can garnish with chopped scallions. Enjoy!

Vegan Cheese Sticks

Servings: 3

Total Time: 8 Hours 40 Minutes

Calories: 116

Fat: 4.1 g

Protein: 12.7 g

Carbs: 9.7 g

Ingredients and Quantity

- 1 block vegan mozzarella, sliced into strips
- 1 bag vegan chips
- 1 1/2 cups almond flour
- 2 cups coconut milk
- 1/4 cup nutritional yeast

Direction

1. Put the chips and nutritional yeast in the food

2. processor.

3. Pulse until powdery.

4. Dip each cheese strip in the milk and cover with flour.

5. Dip into the milk again and coat with the powdered chips.

6. Place in the freezer for 8 hours.

7. Add the frozen cheese sticks to the Ninja Foodi basket.

8. Seal the crisping lid.

9. Set it to air crisp.

10. Cook at 380 degrees for 10 minutes.

11. You can serve with vegetable sticks. Enjoy!

Smoked Chickpeas

Servings: 3

Total Time: 45 Minutes

Calories: 423

Fat: 10.1 g

Protein: 20.8 g

Carbs: 65.2 g

Ingredients and Quantity

- 15 oz. chickpeas, rinsed and drained
- 1 tbsp. sunflower oil
- 2 tbsp. smoked paprika
- 1/2 tsp. granulated garlic
- 1/2 tsp. ground cumin
- 1/4 tsp. granulated onion
- Salt, to taste

Direction

1. Mix all the ingredients except the oil and chickpeas.
2. Put the chickpeas in the Ninja Foodi basket.
3. Seal the crisping lid.
4. Set it to air crisp function.
5. Cook at 390 degrees F for 15 minutes, shaking halfway through.
6. Put the chickpeas in the bowl of seasonings.
7. Put them back to the Ninja Foodi basket.
8. Cook at 360 degrees F for 3 minutes.
9. You can add cayenne pepper to make the dish spicier. Enjoy!

Fried Broccoli

Servings: 2

Total Time: 25 Minutes

Calories: 197

Fat: 14.5 g

Protein: 7.4 g

Carbs: 14.4 g

Ingredients and Quantity

- 4 cups broccoli florets
- 2 tbsp. coconut oil
- 1 tbsp. nutritional yeast
- Salt and pepper, to taste

Direction

1. Combine all the ingredients in a bowl.

2. Place the broccoli in the Ninja Foodi basket.

3. Seal the crisping lid.

4. Choose air crisp setting.

5. Cook at 370 degrees F for 5 minutes.

6. You can serve as side dish. Enjoy!

Garlic Pepper Potato Chips

Servings: 2

Total Time: 30 Minutes

Calories: 197

Fat: 14.5 g

Protein: 7.4 g

Carbs: 14.4 g

Ingredients and Quantity

- 1 large potato, sliced into thin chips
- Cooking spray
- Salt and garlic powder, to taste
- 1 tsp. black pepper

Direction

1. Spray oil on the Ninja Foodi basket.

2. Season the potato with the salt, garlic powder and black pepper.
3. Place potato chips on the basket.
4. Seal the crisping lid.
5. Set it to air crisp.
6. Cook at 450 degrees F for 10 minutes or until golden and crispy.
7. You can serve with mayo dip. Enjoy!

Crispy Brussels Sprouts

Servings: 4

Total Time: 30 Minutes

Calories: 139

Fat: 5.4 g

Protein: 7.8 g

Carbs: 20.9 g

Ingredients and Quantity

- 1 lb. Brussels sprouts
- 2 tbsp. olive oil
- 1/4 tsp. garlic powder
- 1/4 tsp. salt

Direction

1. Put the Brussels sprouts in a bowl.

2. Pour the olive oil into the bowl.

3. Season the sprouts with garlic powder and salt.

4. Put the sprouts on the basket.

5. Seal the crisping lid.

6. Set it to air crisp function.

7. Cook at 370 degrees F for 6 minutes, flipping halfway through.

8. 8. You can serve as side dish. Enjoy!

Veggie Fritters

Servings: 6

Total Time: 45 Minutes

Calories: 171

Fat: 0.5 g

Protein: 5.8 g

Carbs: 35.7 g

Ingredients and Quantity

- 3 tbsp. ground flaxseed mixed with 1/2 cup water
- 2 potatoes, shredded
- 2 cups frozen mixed veggies
- 1 cup frozen peas, thawed
- 1/2 cup onion, chopped
- 1/4 cup fresh cilantro, chopped
- 1/2 cup almond flour
- Salt, to taste
- Cooking spray

Direction

1. Combine all the ingredients in a bowl and then form patties.
2. Spray each patty with oil.
3. Transfer to the Ninja Foodi basket.
4. Set it to air crisp.
5. Close the crisping lid.
6. Cook at 360 degrees F for 15 minutes, flipping halfway through.
7. Transfer to a serving plate. Serve and enjoy!

Steamed Broccoli and Carrots with Lemon

Servings: 3

Total Time: 10 Minutes

Calories: 35

Fat: 0.3 g

Protein: 1.7 g

Carbs: 8.1 g

Ingredients and Quantity

- 1 cup broccoli florets
- 1/2 cup carrots, julienned
- 2 tbsp. lemon juice
- Salt and pepper, to taste

Direction

1. Place the Ninja Foodi Cook and Crisp reversible rack inside the ceramic pot.
2. Pour water into the pot.
3. Toss everything in a mixing bowl and combine.
4. Place the vegetables on the reversible rack.
5. Close the pressure lid and set the vent to SEAL.
6. Press the Steam button and adjust the cooking time to 10 minutes.
7. Do a quick pressure, release. Serve and enjoy!

Crusty Sweet Potato Hash

Servings: 4

Total Time: 15 Minutes

Calories: 195

Fat: 6 g

Protein: 3.7 g

Carbs: 31.4 g

Ingredients and Quantity

- 2 large sweet potatoes, cut into small cubes
- slices bacon, cut into small pieces
- 2 tbsp. olive oil
- 1 tbsp. smoked paprika
- 2 tsp. salt
- 1 tsp. ground black pepper
- tsp. dill weed

Direction

1. Place in the ceramic pot the Ninja Foodi Cook and Crisp basket.
2. Combine all ingredients in a bowl and give a good stir.
3. Form small patties using your hands.
4. Place the patties in the basket.
5. Close the crisping lid and press the Air Crisp button before pressing the START button.
6. Adjust the cooking time to 10 minutes.
7. Flip the patties halfway through the cooking time for even cooking. Serve and enjoy!

Cardamom Tofu Mix

Servings: 4

Total Time: 20 Minutes

Calories: 133

Fat: 7.9 g

Protein: 7.1 g

Carbs: 10.5 g

Fiber: 2 g

Ingredients and Quantity

- 10 oz. firm tofu, cubed
- 1 tsp. lemongrass, minced
- 1 tbsp. lime juice
- 1 tsp. turmeric powder
- 2 sweet potatoes, chopped
- 1 tsp. garlic powder
- 1 tbsp. olive oil

- 1/2 cup almond yogurt

- 1 tsp. ground cardamom
- 1/2 tsp. salt
- 1 tsp. pumpkin seeds
- 1/4 cup water
- 1 tsp. diced garlic
- 1/2 cup fresh cilantro, chopped

Direction

1. Toss the oil in the instant pot and heat up.

2. Then add cubed tofu, lemongrass, turmeric, garlic powder and cardamom and sauté for 3 minutes.

3. Add the rest of the ingredients and toss.

4. Close the lid and sauté for 7 minutes more.

5. Then transfer cooked meal in the serving bowls. Serve and enjoy!

Chili and Lime Cauliflower

Servings: 6

Total Time: 19 Minutes

Calories: 156

Fat: 2.5 g

Protein: 2.1 g

Carbs: 7.8 g

Fiber: 2.6 g

Ingredients and Quantity

- 1 pound cauliflower head
- 1 tsp. garlic powder
- 1 tsp. ground black pepper
- 1 tsp. salt
- 1 tbsp. avocado oil
- 1 tsp. curry powder
- 1 tsp. oregano, dried

- 1 tsp. chili flakes
- 1 tbsp. lime juice
- 1 tsp. coriander
- 1 red onion, roughly chopped
- 1 cup water
- 1 tsp. cayenne pepper

Direction

1. In a bowl, mix the cauliflower with the water, lime juice and the other ingredients and rub well.
2. Transfer the mix to the instant pot.
3. Close and seal the instant pot lid. Cook the meal for 5 minutes on high-pressure mode.
4. Then allow natural pressure release for 5 minutes more.
5. Transfer the cooked cauliflower in the bowl, separate florets.

6. Divide between plates and serve with cooking juices on top. Enjoy!

Chili Tofu

Servings: 2

Total Time: 25 Minutes

Calories: 183

Fat: 8.3 g

Protein: 12.8 g

Carbs: 4.7 g

Fiber: 1.4 g

Ingredients and Quantity

- 10 oz. firm tofu, cubed
- 1 tbsp. soy sauce
- 1 tsp. curry powder
- 1 tsp. balsamic vinegar
- tbsp. fish sauce
- 1 tsp. olive oil
- 1 tsp. dried parsley
- 1 tsp. tomato paste

- 1/2 tsp. chili flakes

Direction

1. In the instant pot mix the tofu with the soy sauce, curry powder and the other ingredients and toss gently.
2. After this, preheat instant pot on Sauté mode.
3. Cook the meal for 2 minutes from each side.
4. Transfer the cooked tofu in the serving bowls and let it chill to room temperature. Serve and enjoy!

Popcorn Broccoli

Servings: 2

Total Time: 17 Minutes

Calories: 153

Fat: 5.8 g

Protein: 3.5 g

Carbs: 6.7 g

Fiber: 2.4 g

Ingredients and Quantity

- 1/2 cup broccoli florets
- 1 tsp. turmeric
- 1 tsp. curry powder
- 1/4 cup almond flour
- 4 tbsp. coconut cream
- 1 tsp. salt
- 1 tsp. black pepper

- 1 tbsp. bread crumbs

- 1 cup water, for cooking

Direction

1. In the mixing bowl combine together the broccoli with turmeric and the other ingredients except bread crumbs and water and toss well.
2. Sprinkle the popcorn broccoli with the bread crumbs.
3. Pour water in the instant pot and insert rack.
4. Place popcorn into the instant pot pan.
5. Transfer the pan on the rack. Close and seal the lid.
6. Cook cauliflower popcorn for 7 minutes on manual mode (high pressure).
7. When the time is over, use quick pressure release.

1. Open the lid and chill the meal to room temperature. Serve and enjoy!

Paprika Todu

Servings: 6

Total Time: 35 Minutes

Calories: 72

Fat: 2.1 g

Protein: 4.6 g

Carbs: 9.6 g

Fiber: 1.6 g

Ingredients and Quantity

- 2 oz. vegetable stock
- 1 tsp. tomato paste
- 5 oz. firm tofu, roughly cubed
- 2 tbsp. sweet paprika
- 1 tsp. coriander, ground
- 1/2 tsp. minced garlic
- 1/2 tsp. white pepper

- 1 tsp. coconut oil

Direction

1. In the instant pot, mxi the tofu with the paprika and the other ingredients and toss gently. Close and seal the lid.

2. Set Sauté mode and cook the meal for 10 minutes.

3. Use natural pressure release for 10 minutes.

4. Divide into bowls and serve. Enjoy!

Lime Spring Onions

Servings: 4

Total Time: 20 Minutes

Calories: 43

Fat: 0.8 g

Protein: 2.2 g

Carbs: 10.7 g

Fiber: 3.2 g

Ingredients and Quantity

- 1 pound spring onions
- 1 tbsp. olive oil
- 1/2 tsp. basil, dried
- 1 tsp. dried cilantro
- 1/2 tsp. salt
- 1/2 tsp. black pepper
- 1 tbsp. lime juice

Direction

1. In the instant pot, mix the spring onions with the basil, oil and the other ingredients.

2. Toss and cook on Sauté mode for 2 minutes for each side.

3. The spring onions are cooked when they are tender but not soft. Serve and enjoy!

Cardamom Stuffed Figs

Servings: 4

Total Time: 12 Minutes

Calories: 101

Fat: 4.8 g

Protein: 1.6 g

Carbs: 14.1 g

Fiber: 2.1 g

Ingredients and Quantity

- 4 figs
- 1/2 tsp. brown sugar
- 3 tbsp. water
- 1/4 tsp. nutmeg, ground
- 4 tsp. coconut butter
- 1 pinch ground cardamom
- 1/2 cup water, for cooking

Direction

1. Crosscut the figs and remove a small amount of fig flesh.
2. Then mix up together the butter with sugar, cardamom and nutmeg.
3. Stir and fill the figs with the cashew butter mixture.
4. Then place them in the instant pot pan.
5. Pour ½ cup of water in the instant pot and insert trivet.
6. Place pan with figs on the trivet. Close and seal the lid.
7. Set Manual mode (high pressure) and cook figs for 2 minutes.
8. Then use quick pressure release.
9. Open the lid and pour the figs with the sweet juice from them.
10. The main dish should be served hot or warm. Enjoy!

Thai Coconut Clams

Servings: 6

Total Time: 30 Minutes

Calories: 343

Fat: 12 g

Protein: 36 g

Carbs: 17 g

Fiber: 3 g

Ingredients and Quantity

- 3 shallots, sliced
- 1 tbsp. coconut oil
- 1 stalk fresh lemongrass, peeled, smashed and minced
- 1/2 cup vegetable broth
- 1 piece (1 inch) fresh ginger, minced
- 2 jalapeno peppers, seeded and sliced

- 2 tbsp. Asian fish sauce
- 1 tbsp. light brown sugar

- 1/2 cup low-fat coconut milk
- 2 pounds clams, scrubbed
- 1 tsp. salt
- 1 tsp. black pepper
- 1 scallion, chopped
- 1/2 fresh cilantro, chopped
- 1 lime, juiced

Direction

1. Press "Sauté" function and add the coconut oil to your Instant Pot.
2. Once the oil is hot, add the shallots and cook for 3 to 5 minutes or until browned, stirring occasionally.
3. Add the lemongrass, stock, ginger, jalapenos, fish sauce, and brown sugar. Allow simmering for 1 minute or until the brown sugar dissolves.
4. Stir in the coconut milk and allow to simmer until thickened, about 5 minutes.

5. Stir in the clams, salt, and black pepper.
6. Close and lock the lid and cook at low pressure for 1 minute.
7. When the cooking is done, naturally release the pressure and remove the lid.
8. Spoon the clams into serving bowls and ladle some broth over them.
9. Garnish with scallions, cilantro and fresh lime juice. Serve and enjoy!

Coconut Curry Sea Bass

Servings: 3

Total Time: 20 Minutes

Calories: 413

Fat: 35.7 g

Protein: 16.8 g

Carbs: 11 g

Fiber: 3.7 g

Ingredients and Quantity

- 1 pound sea bass, cut into 1 inch pieces
- 1 can (14.5 oz.) coconut milk
- 1 lime juice
- 1 tbsp. red curry paste
- 1 tsp. fish sauce
- 1 tsp. coconut aminos
- 1 tsp. maple syrup

- 2 tsp. Sriracha
- 2 garlic cloves, minced
- 1 tsp. ground turmeric
- 1 tsp. ground ginger
- 1/2 tsp. salt
- 1/2 tsp. white pepper
- 1/4 cup cilantro, freshly chopped
- 3 lime wedges

Direction

1. Add the coconut milk, red curry paste, fish sauce, coconut aminos, maple syrup, sriracha, minced garlic, ground turmeric, ground ginger, salt, and pepper in your Instant Pot. Whisk until well combined.
2. Place the sea bass in your Instant Pot and spoon the coconut milk mixture over.
3. Lock the lid and cook at high pressure for 3 minutes.
4. When the cooking is done, quick release the pressure and remove the lid.

5. Transfer the fish and broth to serving bowls.

6. Garnish with cilantro and lime wedges. Serve and enjoy!

Salmon with Chili Lime Sauce

Servings: 2

Total Time: 15 Minutes

Calories: 400

Fat: 25 g

Protein: 29 g

Carbs: 10.5 g

Fiber: 0.5 g

Ingredients and Quantity

- 2 (95 oz.) salmon fillets
- 1 cup water
- 1 tsp. salt
- 1 tsp. black pepper

For Chili-Lime Sauce:

- 1 jalapeno, seeded and chopped
- 1 lime, juiced
- 2 garlic cloves, minced
- 1 tbsp. maple syrup
- 1 tbsp. olive oil
- 1 tbsp. water
- 1 tbsp. parsley, freshly chopped
- 1/2 tsp. paprika
- 1/2 tsp. cumin

Direction

1. In a bowl, add all the chili-lime sauce ingredients. Mix until well combined.
2. Add 1 cup of water and a steam rack inside your Instant Pot.
3. Season your salmon fillets with salt and pepper.
4. Place the salmon fillets on top of the steam rack.
5. Lock the lid and cook at high pressure for 5 minutes.
6. When the cooking is done, quick release the pressure and remove the lid.

7. Drizzle the salmon fillets with the chili-lime sauce. Serve and enjoy!

Coconut Fish Curry

Servings: 6

Total Time: 20 Minutes

Calories: 474

Fat: 35.3 g

Protein: 18.7 g

Carbs: 25 g

Fiber: 2.6 g

Ingredients and Quantity

- 1 1/2 pounds fish fillets, cut into bite-sized pieces
- 1 tomato, chopped
- 2 green chilies, sliced
- 2 garlic cloves, crushed
- 1 tbsp. olive oil
- 1 tbsp. ginger, freshly grated
- 6 curry leaves

- 1 tbsp. ground coriander
- 2 tsp. ground cumin
- 1/2 tsp. ground turmeric
- 1 tsp. chili powder
- 1/2 tsp. ground fenugreek
- 3 tbsp. curry powder
- 2 cups unsweetened coconut milk
- 2 tsp. salt
- 1/2 lemon, squeezed

Direction

1. Press "Sauté" function on your Instant Pot and add the olive oil.
2. Add the curry leaves and allow to simmer until golden around the edges.
3. Add the onions, garlic, and ginger.
4. Cook until the onions have softened, stirring occasionally.
5. Add the coriander, cumin, turmeric, chili powder and fenugreek and cook for 2 minutes or until the aroma is released.

6. Stir in the coconut milk, green chilies, tomatoes and fish pieces. Lock the lid and cook at low pressure for 5 minutes.

7. When the cooking is done, naturally release the pressure and remove the lid.

8. Season with salt and squeeze the lemon. Serve and enjoy!

Garlic Salmon and Asparagus

Servings: 3

Total Time: 9 Minutes

Calories: 343

Fat: 21.2 g

Protein: 33.2 g

Carbs: 8.9 g

Fiber: 3.8 g

Ingredients and Quantity

- 1 pound salmon fillets, cut into 3 equal pieces
- 1pound asparagus, cut into bite-sized pieces
- 1/4 cup lemon juice
- 3 tbsp. almond butter1 1/2 tbsp. garlic, minced
- 1 tsp. salt
- 1/4 tsp. red pepper flakes
- 2 cups water

Direction

1. Lay 3 large pieces of foil on a flat surface.

2. Place 1 salmon piece on each foil.

3. Spread 1/2 tbsp. of garlic on each piece of salmon.

4. Divide and place the asparagus equally between the 3 plates.

5. Sprinkle salt and red pepper flakes on top of each salmon fillet.

6. Add 1 tablespoon of butter on each salmon fillet.

7. Tightly wrap the foil and make sure no steam can escape.

8. Add 2 cups of water and a trivet to your Instant Pot.

9. Place the foil packets on top of the trivet.

10. Lock the lid and press "Steam" function and set for 4 minutes.

11.   When the cooking is done, quick release the

pressure and remove the lid.

12.   Remove the foil packets and open. Transfer

the contents to a plate. Serve and enjoy!

Fish and Potato Chowder

Servings: 8

Total Time: 30 Minutes

Calories: 348

Fat: 22.5 g

Protein: 25 g

Carbs: 13.3 g

Fiber: 2.9 g

Ingredients and Quantity

- 2 1/2 cups fish stock or water
- 1 1/2 pounds tilapia, cut into bite sized pieces
- 1 pound potatoes, chopped
- 1 cup celery, chopped
- 1 cup onions, chopped
- 6 bacon slices, chopped
- 1 1/2 cup unsweetened coconut cream

- 3 tbsp. almond butter
- 1/2 tsp. garlic powder

- 1 tsp. salt
- 1 tsp. black pepper

Direction

1. Press "Sauté" function on your instant pot and add the bacon.

2. Cook until brown and crispy.

3. Remove the bacon and set aside.

4. Add the butter, onions and celery.

5. Cook until the onions have softened, stirring frequently.

6. Add the fish stock, tilapia pieces, salt, pepper, garlic powder and coconut cream to your Instant Pot. Give a good stir.

7. Lock the lid and cook at high pressure for 10 minutes.

8. When the cooking is done, naturally release the pressure and remove the lid.

9. Use a potato masher to mash the potatoes until broken down. You can leave chunks if you prefer. Serve and enjoy!

Soy-Free Asian Salmon

Servings: 2

Total Time: 7 Minutes

Calories: 378

Fat: 17.8 g

Protein: 34.5 g

Carbs: 20.8 g

Fiber: 0 g

Ingredients and Quantity

- 2 salmon fillets
- 1 tbsp. coconut oil
- 1 tbsp. brown sugar
- 1 tbsp. coconut aminos
- 2 tbsp. maple syrup
- 1 tbsp. parsley, chopped
- 1 tsp. Paprika

- 1/4 tsp. Ginger

- 1 tsp. sesame seeds

- 1 tsp. Salt
- 1 tsp. black pepper

Direction

1. Press "Sauté" function on your instant pot and add the coconut oil.

2. Once the oil is hot, add the brown sugar and stir until the sugar has dissolved.

3. Stir in the paprika, ginger, coconut aminos and maple syrup.

4. Add the salmon fillets to your Instant Pot and season with salt and pepper.

5. Lock the lid and cook at low pressure for 2 minutes.

6. When the cooking is done, naturally release the pressure for 5 minutes and quick release any remaining pressure.

7. Remove the lid and transfer the salmon fillets to a plate.

8. Spoon and pour some of the broth over the salmon.

9. Sprinkle the fillets with sesame seeds and garnish with parsley.

10. Serve and enjoy!

Salmon, Potatoes and Broccoli

Servings: 2

Total Time: 10 Minutes

Calories: 467

Fat: 31.8 g

Protein: 27.1 g

Carbs: 21.4 g

Fiber: 3.1 g

Ingredients and Quantity

- 1 (4 oz.) salmon fillets
- 1 medium head broccoli, chopped into florets
- 1 potato, chopped into cubes
- 1 shallot, chopped
- 2 garlic cloves, minced
- 3 tbsp. almond butter
- 1 tbsp. coconut oil

- 1/2 cup fish stock
- 1 tbsp. parsley, chopped
- 1 tsp. salt
- 1 tsp. black pepper

Direction

1. Drizzle the coconut oil over the salmon fillet and season with salt and pepper.

2. Press "Sauté" function on your instant pot and add the butter.

3. Once the butter has melted, add the shallot and cook until softened, stirring occasionally.

4. Add the garlic and cook for 1 minute or until fragrant.

5. Add the broccoli, potatoes, and parsley to your Instant Pot.

6. Cook for 2 minutes, stirring occasionally.

7. Add ½ cup of fish stock and a steaming rack to your Instant Pot.

8. Place the salmon fillets on top of the rack.

9. Lock the lid and cook at high pressure for 4 minutes.

10. When the cooking is done, naturally release the pressure and remove the lid.

11. Transfer the salmon fillet to a plate along with the broccoli and potato mixture. Serve and enjoy!

Shrimp Scampi

Servings: 4

Total Time: 14 Minutes

Calories: 213

Fat: 13 g

Protein: 24 g

Carbs: 1 g

Fiber: 1.6 g

Ingredients and Quantity

- 4 tbsp. almond butter
- 1 tbsp. lemon juice
- 1 tbsp. garlic, minced
- 2 tsp. red pepper flakes
- 1 tbsp. chopped chives or 1 tsp. dried chives
- 1 tbsp. basil leaves, minced (plus more for sprinkling), or 1 tsp. dried basil

- 2 tbsp. chicken stock or white wine
- 1 lb. defrosted shrimp (21 to 25 count)

Direction

1. Turn your air fryer to 330°F. Place a 6 x 3 metal pan in it and allow the oven to start heating while you gather your ingredients.
2. Place the butter, garlic, and red pepper flakes into the hot 6-inch pan.
3. Allow it to cook for 2 minutes, stirring once, until the butter has melted. Do not skip this step. This is what infuses garlic into the butter, which is what makes it all taste so good.
4. Open the air fryer, add all ingredients to the pan in the order listed, stirring gently.
5. Allow shrimp to cook for 5 minutes, stirring once. At this point, the butter should be well-melted

and liquid, bathing the shrimp in spiced goodness.

6. Mix very well, remove the 6-inch pan using silicone mitts and let it rest for 1 minute on the counter. You're doing this so that you let the shrimp cook in the residual heat, rather than letting it accidentally overcook and become rubbery.

7. Stir at the end of the minute. The shrimp should be well cooked at this point.

8. Sprinkle additional fresh basil leaves and enjoy!

Red Cabbage Salad

Servings: 4

Total Time: 10 Minutes

Calories: 110

Fat: 1 g

Protein: 1.1 g

Carbs: 6 g

Fiber: 2.2 g

Ingredients and Quantity

- 1/4 cup white onion, finely chopped
- 2 tsp. red wine vinegar
- 2 cups red cabbage, shredded
- 1 tbsp. canola oil
- Salt and black pepper, to taste
- 1/2 tsp. palm sugar

Direction

1. Put shredded cabbage in your instant pot and add some water.

2. Cover and cook on High for 5 minutes.

3. Release pressure naturally.

4. Drain water and transfer it to a salad bowl.

5. Add salt, pepper to taste, onion, oil, palm sugar and vinegar.

6. Toss to coat. Serve and enjoy right away!

Lightning Source UK Ltd.
Milton Keynes UK
UKHW020742260521
384401UK00005B/93